Threats of Intimacy

Ela Przybylo

BuschekBooks
Ottawa

Library and Archives Canada Cataloguing in Publication

Przybylo, Ela, 1985-
    Threats of intimacy / Ela Przybylo.

Poems.
ISBN 978-1-894543-50-7

    I. Title.
PS8631.R99T47 2008   C811'.6   C2008-906143-8

Cover image: *Wheat Field Sunset*, Copyright © Tye
Carnelli. Available from iStockphoto, File number:
6698956.

Printed by Hignell Book Printing, Winnipeg, Manitoba,
Canada.

BuschekBooks
P.O. Box 74053, 5 Beechwood Avenue
Ottawa, Ontario, K1M 2H9 Canada

BuschekBooks gratefully acknowledges the support
of the Canada Council for the Arts for its publishing
program.

**Canada Council   Conseil des Arts
for the Arts   du Canada**

To my parents for their love,
my sisters for their friendship,
and especially to E.D. Blodgett and Aleksandra Przybylo for
believing in my words.

After sleepless nights
my soul drifts from road to bloom.
Straight, straight
adjacent to the horizon,
my road, my life,
purple glistening asphalt.
Above is the bloom, the fuming sky,
the illusive puff of cloud,
this is the playpen of my poetry.
After sleepless nights
my worlds unwind, unfurl,
and are reflected in one another.
Skies flatten, horizon fades,
purple road reflects the bloom.

After sleepless nights
I scramble from knowing to writing.
Etching words and words
on flat surfaces,
seeking cover from their droning.
These are the clusters of words
that are born,
out of sky, out of road,
out of sleepless nights.

I reduce great efforts to mindless blows.
Withdrawal.
Inferiority striving, striving, seeking.
Damage beyond repair.

Sparrows encircling in search
of that which joyous creatures had formed,
nursed
lost, lost.

Now I balance a grieving being
shaking off its layers
realizing it was only ever me
barehanded.

I awoke enthralled in concupiscence
my bones stinging with hopeful anticipation
my back arching a stretch
and toes gnawing in states of frenzy

I articulated the desire,
the removed essence
Discovered at its core:
a hunger for the sky
a longing to sprout fresh branches
and to be taken by the wind

Without notice
I never recorded absorption
or realms of insatiable curiosity

With one finger raised
in monumental fashion
I retreated to those areas
most common
in slumber.

I will tilt my head
for you
today
allow it to hang on to its last fibres —
for you

For myself I will design a testimony
promises of change and anti-change
languages of repression
curses of optimism

Tomorrow I will resist
the pleas offered by society
to create masochistic gashes
in my upper arms
and fill them with
particles of salt

But today I will surrender
only to remind myself
why I created my island

I choose my pompous flowers
my daily hours;
so much time in between and ahead

Where to go with memories
coated in sugar?

At the end of an hour
when the last minute is folding in
I embellish the thought
of someone following me
to catch my tears
and collect them for necklaces
Perhaps many someones invested in me?

Where to go when flowers wilt
and armpits sweat
all that is potentially useful?
Where to go when my string of tears collapses?
When I find no empathy to offer to my past?
Where to go when the word 'enough'
is materializing itself
on my coat collar

A moment when I enjoy curling up
on the windowsill
ice water in my insides
searching for that final puzzle piece
to complete incompletion

May there not be a feeling of silent fulfillment?
when sitting on the brink of extinction
I feel the under workings of the moon
and my favourite vegetables coexist,
juicy carrots whisper—
they are freed of their cocoons

Restless flies
carefully raise their legs
in processional dance
Perhaps I'm restless?
And in effect they change their form for me
glimmers of sensation
they never lie
sincere like the sun
engulfed by other concerns

Where do we go when we grow old?
Our body melts towards some force in the ground
magnetic perhaps
(I am not oriented in the factors)

Beauty fades
I will accept this

Where does our mind go?
Does it enter into a state of hibernation,
so that it may awake renewed?
Does it expire?

Fingers quench for hydration
like snakes in a desert
nestled in caves
Fingers also hibernating?

Where do we go when we grow old?
Is it an escape at last?
A chaos that silences all outer hectic realms
Or maybe at last an inner dance?
Attracting butterflies with lack of ambitions
preparation for the ultimate deconditioning
silence before silence

Where will I go
when my feet carry me nowhere?
And my hands no longer obedient,
design no illusions of escape?

Pray to me
sorceress
reverse the roles for once
privilege me—your follower
for following
and seeking
like you indicated

Consider me expired
only if I fold my arms
behind my head,
and even then my eyes may glimmer
indicating vain memories of self

This time I will watch and observe
see how you manipulated me
grew me in a vessel
matured me in a pot of geraniums
I never knew your reasons

I desired desperately to discover your truth
take one step through the door
and listen with all my crawling fingers
and eyes
for changes, alterations
in your breathing
gasping

Beg me for once sorceress
to free *your* manacles
Unconsciously—
in the process of placing me in this trap
you have also established your own prison
and carelessly slipped me the key

Now, without the urge
I—the fool
have learned how to fool

Lingering on a fine line
Wishing another would swallow me up
Are all humans fundamentally lonely?
Poplars nod
They are connected by a root system
And they nod.

A day over.
Over the valleys.
Over the burned land.
Over.
Over—the defined extended moment that is a day
—has been completed.
Decorated with dots in commemoration.
Singular dots (not sequences) commemorating the end.
Scabs of sentiments are left to freckle my body.
They envelop every movement, cradle every thought, a
delicate stream.
August has passed.

Be wary of fingertips
they are messages captivated, encapsulated
lined up patiently in rows
begging to be released

Be conscious of these legs
they are tapeworms
awaiting the moment when they will crawl
under your skin
and vitiate your current you
corrupt your process of liberation

Be careful then of the hips
they are algebra equations
that may explode at any given 'if'
with the correct systematic code

Give heed to these nostrils of mine
voids waiting to be filled to their brims
with your scents

When you assume you are safe
restful
consider again
all the threats surrounding you

The body's vulnerability is a show
in that, also a component of the truth
Regardless, my aggressive physical components
are always sincere in their actions

Driven by typical fright and thirst
they will recoil
shattering the margins of sanity
they surprise even me —
who controls them
Always be wary of the threats of intimacy.

I fell in love
with a tree
today
stem cells anchored me
tree's bark anchored me
insomnia of spring

My scent remains on the tree
a trace of the affair's presence
while the evening bleeds

One choleric woman
standing
laughing
leaning so as to emphasize
the laughing
insanely indiscreet
and undirected
spreading, a poisoned gull,
over waste-filled water

Clock ticking rhythmically
Here I am
with my hair—a dead limb
hanging
along with everything
along with yesterday
Yes, yesterday those stones
were drenched with portentous signals
Today they fade off into the background
and all distant notes speak of isolation
alive and preserved like cherries
soaked in syrup waiting to be desired

And so the salt liquefied
(could it have?)
without my knowing why

The moment painted
on the edges of my soul
inscribing the present
on ageless material

The hands drawing
hectic circles
on uninhabited territory
lips trembling, searching
for expression

Surrounding figures
dully humming
to create atmosphere

And the figurative heart—
still
As so often,
very still

Separate me from my breathing
from my flesh
Disembody my essence
Please
Store me in a contained jar
away from fire
and clear its surface of dust
When an opportune moment arises
forget my distorted hands
my rigid palms
my foolish fingernails
Please forget all figures and images and idols
Ignore all thoughts
Only sense crystallized hungers

I salvage any memories
repertoires, grains of ivory
golden imitations
force myself into consecutive realms
where tears fall up
and sounds never are heard
by their creator
no empty champagne bottles
none

I am always turning with my head high
pointed towards horizons
which exist only in their context

I carry minute beads
scatter them
forget them
swallow each one individually
Then, when I begin to choke
I curl into myself
containing withered flowers
I shrink and slither away

Tomorrow I will blossom
a thousand times over
in a dancing maze
I will embrace my shadows

Never sampled blue cigarettes
as much as I had wished to
desired desperately
to experience
their colour
and become
addicted
solely to their colour
blindly
my turn to salvage myself

Still
unhappy
after as preceding
intoxication
similar gray tones
distributed unevenly
gradual shifts
and impetuous evident ones
my skull
imprinted
with these latter
life—still, unhappy
a state

Shadows extend
parallel
to my soul
a chorus of
sun's warmth on imperfect skin

Waiting, waiting
for constellations to align
with this tramway of wakefulness
this blinding shadow of wakefulness

Cars travelling in reverse
are backdrops to longings
too soon dispatched
to new subterranean landscapes
their glimmer seals passion
under the lemon rind moon

Falling asleep
the sky was orange
predecessor to the gleaming
white of snow
imagining the horizon
it must have been blurred
out of vision
lack of light
encroaching winter
flicker of transient forms

Lying alongside
each other
streamlined
corrugated bodies
have not discovered
they personify
demure sunbathing crocodiles
seeking rest ·
with this illness of oblivion
sore backs may merge

Metaphorical heart
had given rise to long stemmed roses
fed by symbolical tears
since you began framing my day
noon to night
night to dawn
the shapes of your facial features
drawn out in the sun's daily repentance
stemmed roses punctuating
our wordless poem
hypothetical romance
metaphorical lust

Ringing bells
of a landscape
controlled by weather, sun

An insect bitten arm swells, heals
wisdom of that insect transferred

The articulate premonition
of a snail in a shell
also integrated into the landscape

The landscape is my body's prayer,
it rejects my company

Do you find me beautiful
when I am emitting
my concave fears
with my soul
over the daily vessel?
Or when I curl over
to speak to my toes
addressing them as my familiars?
Is there poetic prose in my movements
with movement's retreat
is there a quest to find more stillness yet?
I would like to know.
And be oriented in the fluidity
that transmits under our eyes
under our observation
Do you find me beautiful, then?
Thoughts dance in your direction

In my both hands
a bubble, an orb
ephemeral, unnameable
as still as fire
tingling with warmth
luminescent
as I try to absorb more vocabulary
it shines

My feet have grown claws
spawning into the soil
rooting me
the bubble shifts
in my hand
and observes
and absorbs
I stand and stand
immovable
time is gone
as it always was

Spoonfuls of sun,
tiles, dripping walls,
words that bounce,
the immaculate sun—
predecessor to human inaptitude,
removed observer

Mind curled into my tonsils
inimitability of sleep on my tongue
I dress warmly
my nothingness will be very beautiful

Under-sanctified
gray ocean
vice, vice
of chlorine
resound my tragic cataclysms
amplify this loss of tide

Body is asleep
and I remain on the edge
of the ebb

Somnolent body
gone, gone
soaked into high tide sand
soaked through prehistoric crust

My body lies
away from me
its presence felt through the collective memory

I am inverted and alone
while my body waits and lingers
not assailing
not demanding
I am a wisp of crashing wave

Pain,
my pain
reflected in sky and sun
rendering me more immense
the word, itself is spent
lingering longer than it asks to
'pain'
meet extinction with dignity

Life flush left
rosy Virginia's cheek
of cranberry cocktails
that stained her lips in silence

Birth rights of shut doors
and wholesome vacuums
grazing indoors
shield Virginia from emotional outskirts
so safe, so sweet
Virginia slumbers

What is left in this world but apathy?
And the reluctance to stray away,
and the fear of writing sentences?
What if they stray?
Filtrated phrases
recorded words
regurgitated back and forth throughout
the history of literacy
contradictions clear as rain
Along with hallucinations of small people
who offer water and reasonable things
a little skiff over a never populated pond
wailing harpoons of the ambulance
yet the truth floats, exuberantly glowing,
mischievous

I have time
I have time
Where will I place it?
How will I hold it?

Today curls and strangles
Today vomits
Today I caress time
And it escapes

The streets ablaze today
Autumn
The moon revealed four hours after noon
Ribbon on the edge of platform reality
And fiery fiery stars around my feet
Leaves—autumn

My metaphorical heart
Transforming in unison with my physical one
You know that feeling?
Autumn

When time – the concept, the notion, the fight
Is livid with slow slow rage
And we are here with a carpet of remnants
And we are there decorating the heavens
Autumn, autumn, autumn
Blink away the light

A bubble of breath pops
my nose punctuates the landscape red
my skin imitates the night sky
after it has been punctured by
countless fuming stars
and the winter light
on my orange bedcover
a reminder that
not yet
not now

Sombre good evening
time of healthy decay
along with trees
I lose my colour

What appropriate hue
would illuminate this now?
hanging thread
and diminishing space

I like evenings
with all their impurities
and spectrums of blue
they mask my imperfections
overlook my additional formations

Evenings soothe
remind us of our finite meanings

encourage us to store away our present transactions
and diffuse into the horizon

I am my own evening
on certain days
when descending unto myself
I release the knots of reality

Hallucinations of the future
An existence slowing down its momentum

Raging stomachs shrinking in on themselves
intestines braiding,
coiling those memories
when puss flooded out of our fingertips
we were all so fascinated —
before memories could feasibly be recorded
Childhood.

What altered in the following decade?
What shifted?
This is our second childhood
yet we see puss everywhere
a landscape of yellow blotches
and still no emotion
or the wrong emotions

We neglect our fingertips
imagining them too valuable to be
infected
we feign consciousness
and worship our misfortunes

I wish I had the power then
to record, trace, outline
the sensation of an infected finger
a boy's fascination with that finger
and all that illegible time
that led to now

With the urgency
of clustered blood
an inverted tulip dress
lingers on display
wet laundry
on the line outside
frigid from the cold

Days tumble out
loose
dry
the inner winds
of disposable grocery bags
out, out
onto the pavement

And we remain
in wonder
whether they be lost
or enmeshed in molten plastic,
we wonder
until days halt and congeal
then, heads canted,
we will know

Will I stop writing
when my lips are punctured
and the vent of sound is instilled
If I speak, will I ever
interrogate thoughts
embellish impulses
sheathe wandering cadavers?
What is truth
if not withholding belching reality?

Commenting on your meekness
as if an offering
from your holy veins

Chasing rebirth
of snow
the foreign perception of snow
stillness

Some muse you are
whose figure balances
on a winter equilibrium
stroking frozen flesh

Like snow
your essence is not fabricated
the gift
of absence
amplified twofold

There it was
that poeticized summer
infantilised
in its aimless wanderings
affixed to memory's playpen
fields and skies
merging
floating feather
or ephemeral puff of cloud
between the voids
of factual significance
it humbly thrived
coaxing and waning
feathered fields
and ebbing skies

It's almost six
and my breath is almost gone

Fireflies loving my blood,
loving the sky

This drama of breath
illuminated by their souls

It's almost six
and where is my soul?

My breath
a wisp of feather
descending from colourless sky
Where is my soul?

What is a day?
What is a life?
What is a cup?
What is a question?
What is a question?
A cosmic void seeking
like the humming of a headache
to speak.

I think of prairies stretched thin
amorously
they are flat, flat
flatter than reality
alongside Saturn and her rings
Jupiter and his moons
but they are here

While galaxies wander
and suns flame up and burst
prairies lie
under blankets
of punctured blues
with still light hovering
flat ground shivering
myself, noon, and midnight

I still write the rustling of winds
Still see the calming of leaves
Eavesdrop on rain rolling by
And seek the sun's sweat on my skin

Here is motion
There is stillness
Where am I?

Gentlemen
Sailing on my virgin claws
Align your woes
Paint my envy
Paint my flood
Capture the soul
That fluttered, that waned, that dove

Your tongues sip
My souls' gossip
By a roadside stop two miles down
They find and devour

I want to write my tongue
as it drifts from my mouth
with childhood's transparency
and tickle mute infants
while they know that it's talk
decipher that half moon of a lip

This is the sky,
however else
would a finger bloom?

Those parting sighs
tickled my blood
they itched
like sprouting stars.
I offered bouquets
of sunlit skies
I offered everything.

When there was your shoe
as empty and still
as your presence
I fled to those skies
to those stars.

You traced my path
as does the sun
in wake of the moon
as the moon
searches for the sun.

And there I was
that homeless shoe
fleeing from the black
fleeing from the laughter
with a streetlight sighing
breathing out my light.

There will be tomorrow
As there is today
There will be an instance
The sun swaying
On barbed fence
As it buoyantly appears
There will be one hush of sleep
One word that is poetry
Footstep, footstep

I watched
a two-legged deer
scramble across the road
its second half
hanging carcass
fresh and raw
sticking to the pavement

I watched —
myself two-legged —
wondering if its last jump
was higher
or last landing firmer

Up above the moving clouds
the moving time
and yes
there was some love
tattooed just under my throat
also watching

Words simpler
Body whiter
Unchanged sun
Charging
Where does it hide?
Where does it end, if ever?

The seas drift
What will I write?

Air fogs,
sleep seeps away from my fingers

How do we live
knowing that our bones ache
and thoughts swell —
and still
nothing

This illusion of life
sighs alongside death
This is it.

There were sunflowers
in late autumn
still breathing in my room
they were thirsty for an afterlife

Also, burial grounds
under the swaying chestnut tree
knowing only
the decadence of life

Was I asleep in the light of noon?
Searching for something more
beautiful
or more enduring?

Stars below my feet
reflecting those above
and I had never noticed
their secret hum
and transparent longing
their golden bright
amber awe

Our souls
manifested here
our cities and triumphs
pining
for those above
those above are always

My notebooks speak my souls
they are paper and straight long lines
recording my passing, my dwelling
they are bright and expectant
instantly reclining
perceptive
they are my souls
and they are my leaves
disguising my outline

Wrapped in a blue sky,
breathing with its pulse—
this life is less reassuring

A canvas my view
houses sunken oars
branches tapping
against branches
sweet dendron of the underseas

Nothing ever bluer
or more transparent
or closer to my skin
than this evening's lustre
fading, dim

To whom may I write an incantation?
To the devil of dawn
masking in that masculine grin?
Or to the generic kitchen stool
aching to be stroked?

So many times we search
for the colour of gossip
overcome with fury and pleasure
Too many more
we are alone and idle
and loathing what suns may come
what days may bring

I was gone in the night
but today is dawn
today you are more gone
than ever I have been

How raw my lips
How rare the timber

Lit hallway
Growing ring of dark

Silent melancholy
Fingers whisper
No two pains alike

Sip at the orange of the sky
it is only once we taste snow
it is only once we dance

Unravel that moment
before night
when the world is unpredictable
with tomorrow aching

Drink in the night
our last?
our first?
the only one I know.

You'll find me fleeing with the moon
gathering in the filth
of the road
with the sky still hanging

I fall in love easily
transparently blushing within
aching on all sides

I fall in love
with the harbour at passing noon
the crawling clouds
the festering flies
I fall in love also
with cheating sparrows
who never sit still long
who steal my heart
along with mountain ash

I fall in love
when I see that woman
confident in azure dress
or the boy
who is blooming with the snow

I fall in love so often
How could I not fall in love with you?

Is there a place?
Is there any place?
Place all thoughts away
Is there this place?

See—my freckles are darkening
despite my honest efforts
my eyes, too, are waning green

I am candid
I am waiting—
Where?

Been seeing skies
instead of friends
tracing the route of the day
How does motion avoid stillness?
Does the day ever tire?

Our bodies are our greatest gifts
from whom?
from what?
and once we fade
how we will long for them

The sureness of the earth
the impenetrability of the sky
everything we touch or understand

Infinite ice settled on the eye's lashes
numb contact of skin with cold
laughter rising
infatuation fading
the body's shadows

I have been so frugal with mine
born of another epoch
craving only tables and chairs and books

And yet here is enchantment
physicality
consciousness
here is regret

What would I most like to take with me?
The ripple of dawn
clean
spreading
radiant with elusive time

or five leaves in a row
autumn fastened to a page

What would I choose
from among the myriads
of dangers,
from among the slivers penetrating routine?

this instance of choice

My mother
aligns six drinking glasses
vivid red
with their liquid souls
and they wait
and shiver
while our feet sweep the floor
while chairs shuffle
words are thrown
all six know they are waiting
sharing their presence
with each other
the light that disturbs their disguise
disturbs me into believing
they are alive
they stand obediently, skilfully still
knowing there is nothing more

How lovely
the curve of the pavement
as it bends to my feet's dance

Oh how lovely
trees hanging
low
quivering against rooftops
combing hair

There are mornings and middays
vulnerability where hair has been
and skies that are blue or velvet or gray
mild or saturated

And hair remains
drifting through clouds
glowing in sunsets
days after our bodies end

If I do not write
I sink
into the fleshy moonless sky
the one that warns me
against diving across the day
fearless and brute and desperate
I am desperate

Desperation
wheels through my face
and others read me well

When the night is not moon lit
there is no anchor
I am no-where
neither here, materialized, real
among books and things
nor with the moon away

And all my written
wet words
scramble
crawling off the edges of the page

By January
my face stretches thin
pale unloved skin
is starker than the snow
against the densening of the night

Feel myself drawn shut
as a schoolchild's knapsack might be
on the final day of school

Feel myself
feeling the cold
and knowing the cold
and being the cold

January—sometimes cruel
stings me with its chill
persistence of snow-glazed roads
stale car resting in a snow bank
keys misplaced

Unwriting myself
unmapping, unweaving
to some preknowing state
of vibrant foliage
the eve of my days

Some days surface
vibrant and clear
beneath the skin-lip of the calming waters
others melt away
into the technicolour background
the moving moving water mass

I ate salted pistachios
or you did?
but the taste was mine

Sky opened like a valve
with pinpricked marks
washed clean with clouding
and all I knew
was the dense air and denser grass

may I be that starless night
milky pure
with no intersecting points

Simultaneity of
goodbye and hello love
has not wandered far from me

Reading more of my body
than pierces
through wool sweaters
in this Albertan winter frost

Reading more of my body
and reading presence
reading absence
woven, locked, embracing

Anticipating the door
an opening door
(while my teeth pierce
the white inner skin, outer flesh
of this displaced watermelon
far from all it knows)

wait
wait
for the life-lust sonata
to strike